A token for children. Extracted from a late author. By John Wesley, M.A. Ninth edition.

James Janeway

A token for children. Extracted from a late author. By John Wesley, M.A. Ninth edition.
Janeway, James
ESTCID: T175459
Reproduction from John Rylands University Library of Manchester
A late author = James Janeway.
London : printed in the year, 1788.
78p. ; 32°

ECCO

Eighteenth Century Collections Online Print Editions

Gale ECCO Print Editions

Relive history with *Eighteenth Century Collections Online*, now available in print for the independent historian and collector. This series includes the most significant English-language and foreign-language works printed in Great Britain during the eighteenth century, and is organized in seven different subject areas including literature and language; medicine, science, and technology; and religion and philosophy. The collection also includes thousands of important works from the Americas.

The eighteenth century has been called "The Age of Enlightenment." It was a period of rapid advance in print culture and publishing, in world exploration, and in the rapid growth of science and technology – all of which had a profound impact on the political and cultural landscape. At the end of the century the American Revolution, French Revolution and Industrial Revolution, perhaps three of the most significant events in modern history, set in motion developments that eventually dominated world political, economic, and social life.

In a groundbreaking effort, Gale initiated a revolution of its own: digitization of epic proportions to preserve these invaluable works in the largest online archive of its kind. Contributions from major world libraries constitute over 175,000 original printed works. Scanned images of the actual pages, rather than transcriptions, recreate the works ***as they first appeared.***

Now for the first time, these high-quality digital scans of original works are available via print-on-demand, making them readily accessible to libraries, students, independent scholars, and readers of all ages.

For our initial release we have created seven robust collections to form one the world's most comprehensive catalogs of 18th century works.

Initial Gale ECCO Print Editions collections include:

History and Geography

Rich in titles on English life and social history, this collection spans the world as it was known to eighteenth-century historians and explorers. Titles include a wealth of travel accounts and diaries, histories of nations from throughout the world, and maps and charts of a world that was still being discovered. Students of the War of American Independence will find fascinating accounts from the British side of conflict.

Social Science

Delve into what it was like to live during the eighteenth century by reading the first-hand accounts of everyday people, including city dwellers and farmers, businessmen and bankers, artisans and merchants, artists and their patrons, politicians and their constituents. Original texts make the American, French, and Industrial revolutions vividly contemporary.

Medicine, Science and Technology

Medical theory and practice of the 1700s developed rapidly, as is evidenced by the extensive collection, which includes descriptions of diseases, their conditions, and treatments. Books on science and technology, agriculture, military technology, natural philosophy, even cookbooks, are all contained here.

Literature and Language

Western literary study flows out of eighteenth-century works by Alexander Pope, Daniel Defoe, Henry Fielding, Frances Burney, Denis Diderot, Johann Gottfried Herder, Johann Wolfgang von Goethe, and others. Experience the birth of the modern novel, or compare the development of language using dictionaries and grammar discourses.

Religion and Philosophy

The Age of Enlightenment profoundly enriched religious and philosophical understanding and continues to influence present-day thinking. Works collected here include masterpieces by David Hume, Immanuel Kant, and Jean-Jacques Rousseau, as well as religious sermons and moral debates on the issues of the day, such as the slave trade. The Age of Reason saw conflict between Protestantism and Catholicism transformed into one between faith and logic -- a debate that continues in the twenty-first century.

Law and Reference

This collection reveals the history of English common law and Empire law in a vastly changing world of British expansion. Dominating the legal field is the *Commentaries of the Law of England* by Sir William Blackstone, which first appeared in 1765. Reference works such as almanacs and catalogues continue to educate us by revealing the day-to-day workings of society.

Fine Arts

The eighteenth-century fascination with Greek and Roman antiquity followed the systematic excavation of the ruins at Pompeii and Herculaneum in southern Italy; and after 1750 a neoclassical style dominated all artistic fields. The titles here trace developments in mostly English-language works on painting, sculpture, architecture, music, theater, and other disciplines. Instructional works on musical instruments, catalogs of art objects, comic operas, and more are also included.

A TOKEN FOR CHILDREN.

Extracted from a late AUTHOR.

By JOHN WESLEY, M. A.

THE NINTH EDITION.

Suffer little Children to come unto me, and forbid them not, for such is the kingdom of God Luke x. 14.

LONDON:

PRINTED IN THE YEAR 1788.

A

TOKEN

FOR

CHILDREN.

EXAMPLE I.

1 MRS. *SARAH HOWLEY*, when ſhe was between eight and nine years old, was carried by her friends to hear a ſermon where the Miniſter preached upon Matt. xi. 30, *My yoke is eaſy, and my burden is light*: in the applying of which ſcripture, the child was mightily awakened and made deeply ſenſible of the condition of her ſoul, and

her need of Christ, she wept bitterly to think what a case she was in, and went home, got by herself into a chamber, and upon her knees she wept and cried to the Lord, as well as she could, which might easily be perceived by her eyes and countenance.

2 She was not contented with this, but she got her little brother and sister into a chamber with her, and told them their condition by nature, and wept over them, and prayed with them.

3. After this, she heard another sermon upon *Proverbs* xxix. 1, *He that being often reproved, hardeneth his neck, shall suddenly be destroyed, and that without remedy*, at which she was more affected than before, and was so exceeding solicitous about her soul, that she spent great part of the night in weeping and praying, and could scarce take any

rest

reſt day or night nor ſome time together; deſiring with all her ſoul to eſcape from everlaſting flames, and to get an intereſt in the Lord Jeſus O what ſhould ſhe do for Chriſt! what ſhould ſhe do to be ſaved!

4. She gave herſelf much to attending upon the word preached, and ſtill continued very tender under it, greatly reliſhing what ſhe heard.

5. She was very much in ſecret prayer, and was uſually very importunate, and full of tears.

6. She could ſcarce ſpeak of ſin, or be ſpoke to, but her heart was ready to melt

7 She ſpent much time in reading the Scripture

8 She was exceeding dutiful to her parents, very loath to grieve them in the leaſt, and if ſhe had at any time (which was very rare) offended

fended them, ſhe would weep bitterly.

9. She abhorred lying, and allowed herſelf in no known ſin.

10. When ſhe was at ſchool ſhe was eminent for her diligence, teachableneſs, meekneſs and modeſty, ſpeaking a little, but when ſhe did ſpeak, it was uſually ſpiritual.

11. She continued in this courſe of religious duties for ſome years together.

12. When ſhe was about fourteen years old, ſhe broke a vein in her lungs, as is ſuppoſed) and often ſpat blood, yet did a little recover again.

13. At the beginning of January ſhe was taken very bad again, in which ſickneſs ſhe was in great diſtreſs of ſoul. When ſhe was firſt taken, ſhe ſaid, "O mother, pray for me, for Satan is ſo buſy that I cannot pray for myſelf, I ſee I

am

am undone without Chriſt, and a pardon! O I am undone to all eternity!"

14. Her mother knowing how ſerious ſhe had been formerly, did a little wonder that ſhe ſhould be in ſuch agonies, and aſked her what ſin it was that was ſo burthenſome to her ſpirit? O mother ſaid ſhe, it is not any paticular ſin that ſticks ſo cloſe to my conſcience, as the ſin of my nature without the blood of Chriſt that will damn me"

15 Her mother aſked her, what ſhe ſhould pray for, for her? ſhe anſwered, 'That I may have a ſaving knowledge of Jeſus Chriſt: and that I may have an aſſurance of God's love to my ſoul." Her mother aſked her, Why ſhe ſpoke ſo little to the miniſter that came to her? She anſwered "It was her duty with patience and ſilence to learn of him"

16. One time when ſhe fell into a fit, ſhe cried out, "O I am going

I am going: but what ſhall I do to be ſaved? Lord Jeſus, I will lie at thy feet, and if I periſh, it ſhall be at the fountain of thy mercy."

17. She was much afraid of preſumption, and dreaded a miſtake in the matters of her ſoul, and would be often putting up ejaculations to God, to deliver her from deceiving herſelf. To inſtance in one, "Great and mighty God, ſaid ſhe, give me faith and true faith, that I may not be a fooliſh virgin, having a lamp and no oil."

18. Her father bid her be of good cheer, becauſe ſhe was going to a better Father: at which ſhe fell into a great agony, and ſaid, "But how do I know that? I am a poor ſinner that wants aſſurance. O, for aſſurance!" This was her great, earneſt, and conſtant requeſt, to all that came to her, to beg aſſurance for her, and ſhe would look with ſo much

much eagerneſs upon them, as if ſhe deſired nothing in the world ſo much as that they would pity her, and help her with their prayers. Never was a poor creature more earneſt for any thing than ſhe was for aſſurance, and the light of God's countenance O the piteous moan that ſhe would make! O the agonies that her ſoul was in?

19. The Lord's-day before that on which ſhe died, a kinſman of her's came to ſee her, and aſking of her, whether ſhe knew him? She anſwered, 'Yes, I know you and I deſire you would learn to know Chriſt. you are young, but you know not how ſoon you may die! and O to die without Chriſt, is a fearful thing, O redeem time! O time, time, precious time!' Being requeſted by him not to ſpend herſelf. ſhe ſaid, She would fain do all the good ſhe could while ſhe lived: upon which account ſhe

desired that a sermon might be preached at her funeral, concerning the preciousness of time.

20. Some ministers that came to her, did with earnestness beg, that the Lord would please to give her some token for good, that she might go off triumphing; and bills of the same nature were sent to several churches.

21. After she had long waited for an answer of their prayers, she said, *Well, I will venture my soul upon* Christ.

22. For the pains and agonies that she was in, her patience was next to a wonder: "Lord, Lord, give me patience, said she, that I may not dishonour thee!"

23 Upon Thursday after long waiting, great fears, and many prayers, when all her friends thought she had been past speaking to the astonishment of her friends, she broke forth thus, with a very audible voice, and cheerful countenance;

nance; "Lord, thou haſt promiſed that whoſoever comes unto thee, thou wilt in no wiſe caſt him out: Lord, I come unto thee, and ſurely thou wilt in no wiſe caſt me out. O ſo ſweet! O ſo glorious is Jeſus; I have thee, ſweet and glorious Jeſus: he is ſweet, he is ſweet! O the admirable love of God in ſending Chriſt, and free grace to a poor loſt creature!"

24. Her ſoul then ſeemed raviſhed with the love of Chriſt. And while ſhe was engaged in magnifying of God, her father, brethren, and ſiſters, with others of the family, were called, to whom ſhe ſpake particularly, as her ſtrength would give leave. She gave her bible as a legacy to one of her brothers, and deſired him to uſe that well for her ſake, and added, to him and the reſt, "O make uſe of time to get Chriſt for your ſouls: ſpend no time in running up and down, or in play-

in-

ing: O get Christ for your soul while you are young! Remember now your Creator before you come to a sick-bed put not off this great work till then, for then you will find it hard work indeed I know by experience, the devil will tell you it is time enough; and ye are young, what need ye be in such haste? You will have time enough when you are old. But remember the words of a dying sister. If you knew how good Christ were! If you had but one taste of his sweetness, you had rather go to him a thousand times than stay in this wicked world I would not for ten thousand worlds part with my interest in Christ O how happy am I, that I am going to everlasting joys! I would not go back again for twenty thousand worlds, and will you not strive to get an interest in Christ?"

24. After

25. After this, looking upon one of her father's servants, she said, "What shall I do at the great day, when Christ shall say to me, *Come thou blessed of my Father, inherit the kingdom prepared for thee?* And shall say to the wicked, *Go thou cursed into the lake that burns for ever!* What a grief is it for me to think, that I shall see any of my friends that I knew upon earth, turned into that lake that burns for ever! O that word for ever! Remember that, for ever! I speak these words to you, but they are nothing, except God speaks to you too O pray, that God would give you grace!" And then she prayed, "O Lord, finish thy work upon their souls. it will be my comfort to see you in glory, but it will be your everlasting happiness."

26 Upon Friday, after she had had such lively discoveries of God's love, she was exceeding desirous to die, and cried out, "Come, Lord Jesus,

Jeſus, come quickly! conduct me to thy tabernacle. I am a poor creature without thee but Lord Jeſus, my ſoul longs to be with thee: O when ſhall it be? Why not now, dear Jeſus? Come, Lord Jeſus, come quickly! But why do I ſpeak thus? Thy time, dear Lord, is the beſt: O give me patience

27 Upon Saturday ſhe ſpoke but little, (being very drowſy) yet now and then ſhe dropt theſe words, "How long ſweet Jeſus? Finiſh thy work, ſweet Jeſus. come away Lord Jeſus, come quickly"

28 Upon the Lord's-day ſhe ſcarce ſpoke any thing, but much deſired that bills of thankſgiving might be ſent to thoſe who had formerly been praying for her, that they might help her to praiſe God for that full aſſurance that he had given her of his love. and ſeemed to be ſwallowed up with the thoughts of God's free love to her ſoul. She oft commended

mended her spirit into the Lord's hands and the last words which she was heard to speak were these Lord help, Lord Jesus help, dear Lord Jesus, blessed Jesus -- And thus upon the Lord's-day, between nine and ten o'clock in the forenoon, she slept sweetly in Jesus and began an everlasting sabbath, Feb. 19, 1670.

EXAMPLE II.

1. A Little child, whose mother had dedicated him to the Lord in her womb, when he could not speak plain, would be crying after God and was greatly desirous to be taught good things.

2. He could not endure to be put to bed without prayer, but would put his parents upon it, with much devotion kneel down, and with great patience and delight continue till it was at an end, without the least sign of

of being weary. And he ſeemed never ſo well pleaſed as when he was ſo engaged

3. He could not be ſatisfied with family prayer but he would be often upon his knees by himſelf, in one corner or another.

4 He was much delighted in hearing the word of God either read or preached.

5. He loved to go to ſchool, that he might learn ſomething of God, and would take great notice of what he nad read, and come home and ſpeak of it with much affection He would rejoice in his book, and ſay to his mother, "O mother, I had a ſweet leſſon to-day, will you pleaſe to give me leave to fetch my book, that you may hear it?"

6. He quickly learned to read the ſcripture, and would with great reverence, tenderneſs, and groans, read till tears and ſobs were ready to hinder him.

7. When

7. When he was at secret prayer, he would weep bitterly

8. He was wont often to complain of the wickedness of his heart, and seemed to be more grieved for the corruption of his nature, than for actual sin

9 He was much troubled for the wandering of his thoughts in prayer, and that he could not always keep his heart fixed upon God, and his affections constantly raised.

10. He kept a watch over his heart, and observed the workings of his soul, and would complain, that they were so vain and foolish, and so little busied about spiritual things.

11. He was exceeding importunate with God in prayer, and would plead with God at a strange rate, and he would beg and expostulate, and weep so, that sometimes it could not be kept from the ears of the neighbours, so that one in the next

next houfe was forced to cry out, "The prayers and tears of that child in the next houfe will fink me to hell," becaufe by it he did condemn his neglect of prayer, and his flight performance of it.

12. He abhorred lying with his foul

13 When he had committed any fin, he was eafily convinced of it, and would get into fome corner or fecret place and with tears beg pardon of God and ftrength againft it.

14. When other children were playing, he would be praying.

15 A friend of his afked him, when he was firft taken fick, Whether he was willing to die? He anfwered, No, becaufe he was afraid of his ftate as to another world Why, child, faid the other, thou didft pray for a new heart, for a humble and a fincere heart, and I have heard thee: didft thou not pray

pray with thy heart? I hope I did, faid he.

16 Not long after the fame perfon afked him again, Whether he was willing to die? He anfwered, "Now I am willing, for I fhall go to Chrift."

17 He ftill grew weaker and weaker, but behaved with a great deal of fweetnefs and patience, waiting for his change. At laft calling upon the name of the Lord, and faying "Lord Jefus, Lord Jefus!" He fweetly flept, dying when he was between five and fix years old.

EXAMPLE III.

1. MARY A. when fhe was between four and five years old, was greatly affected in hearing the word of God, and became very folicitous about her foul, weeping

bitterly, to think what would become of her in another world, asking strange questions concerning God and Christ, and her own soul. So that before she was full five years old, she minded the one thing needful, and chose the better part.

2 She was wont to be much in secret prayer, and many times came off from her knees with tears.

3. She would chuse such times and places for secret prayer, as might render her less observed by others and endeavoured to conceal what she was doing, when she was engaged therein.

4. Her mother being full of sorrow after the death of her husband, this child came to her and asked her why she wept so exceedingly? Her mother answered, she had cause enough to weep, because her father was dead. "No dear mother, said the child, you have no cause to weep so much, for God is a good God still."

5. She

5 She was a dear lover of faithful ministers One time after ſhe had been hearing of Mr. *Whitaker*, ſhe ſaid, "I love that man dearly for the ſweet words that he ſpeaks concerning Christ"

6 Her book was her delight; and many times ſhe was ſo ſtrangely affected in reading the Scriptures, that ſhe burſt out into tears, and would hardly be pacified ſo greatly was ſhe taken with Chriſt's ſufferings, the zeal of God's ſervants, and the danger of a natural ſtate

7 She complained often of the corruption of her nature, of the hardneſs of her heart that ſhe could repent no more, and be no more humble and grieved for her ſins againſt a good God and when ſhe thus complained, it was with abundance of tears.

8 She was very conſcientious in keeping the Sabbath, ſpending the whole time either in reading or

 praying,

praying, or learning her catechifm, or teaching her brothers or fifters. One time when fhe was left at home upon the Lord's day fhe got fome other little children together, with her brothers and fifters, and told them, That was the Lord's day, and that they ought to remember that day to keep it holy She then told them it was to be fpent in religious exercifes all the day except fo much as was taken up in the works of neceffity and mercy. then fhe prayed with them, and among other things begged, that the Lord would give grace and wifdom to them, (little Children,) that they might know how to ferve him.

9. At another time a near relation of her's, being in fome ftraights, made fome complaint, to whom fhe faid, "I have heard Mr *Garter* fay, A man may go to heaven without a penny in his purfe, but not without grace in his heart."

10. She

10. She had an extraordinary love to the people of God, and when ſhe ſaw any that ſhe thought feared the Lord, her heart would even leap for joy.

11 When ſhe was between eleven and twelve years old ſhe ſickened of the plague, in which ſhe behaved with admirable patience and ſweetneſs, and did what ſhe could with ſcripture arguments to ſupport and encourage her relations to part with her that was going to glory, and to prepare themſelves to meet her in a bleſſed eternity.

12. She was not many days ſick before ſhe was marked, which ſhe firſt ſaw herſelf, and was greatly rejoiced to think that ſhe was marked out for the Lord, and was now going apace to Chriſt. She called to her friends and ſaid, "I am marked, but be not troubled, for I know I am marked for one of the Lord's own."

own." One asked her, how she knew that? She answered, "The Lord hath told me, that I am one of his dear children." And this she spoke with a holy confidence in the Lord's love, and was not in the least daunted at her death but seemed greatly delighted in the apprehension of her nearness to her Father's house. And it was not long before she was filled with joy unspeakable in believing.

13. When she lay a dying, her mother came to her, and told her, she was sorry she had reproved and corrected so good a child so oft. "O mother, said she, speak not thus. I bless God, now I am dying, for your reproofs and corrections too: for, it may be, I might have gone to hell, if it had not been for your reproofs and corrections."

14. Some of her neighbours coming to visit her, asked her if she could leave them? She answered,

"If

"If you ſerve the Lord, you ſh[illegible] come after me to glory."

15. A little before ſhe died, ſhe had a great conflict with Satan, and cried out, "I am none of his." Her mother ſeeing her troubled, aſked her what was the matter? She anſwered, Satan did trouble me, but now, I thank God, all is well I know I am none of his, but Chriſt's.

16. After this, ſhe had a great ſenſe of God's love, and a glorious ſight, as if ſhe had ſeen the very heavens open, and the angels come to receive her, by which her heart was filled with joy, and her tongue with praiſe.

17. Being deſired by the ſtanders-by to give them a particular account of what ſhe ſaw, ſhe anſwered, "you ſhall know hereafter" and ſo in an extaſy of joy and holy triumph ſhe went to God, when ſhe was about twelve years old.

EXAMPLE

own." One aſked her, how ſhe knew that? She anſwered, "The Lord hath told me, that I am one of his dear children." And this ſhe ſpoke with a holy confidence in the Lord's love, and was not in the leaſt daunted at her death; but ſeemed greatly delighted in the apprehenſion of her nearneſs to her Father's houſe. And it was not long before ſhe was filled with joy unſpeakable in believing.

13. When ſhe lay a dying, her mother came to her, and told her, ſhe was ſorry ſhe had reproved and corrected ſo good a child ſo oft. "O mother, ſaid ſhe, ſpeak not thus. I bleſs God, now I am dying, for your reproofs and corrections too: for, it may be, I might have gone to hell, if it had not been for your reproofs and corrections."

14. Some of her neighbours coming to viſit her, aſked her if ſhe could leave them? She anſwered, "If

"If you ſerve the Lord, you ſh[illegible] come after me to glory."

15 A little before ſhe died, ſhe had a great conflict with Satan, and cried out, 'I am none of his." Her mother ſeeing her troubled, aſked her what was the matter? She anſwered, Satan did trouble me, but now, I thank God, all is well I know I am none of his, but Chriſt's.

16 After this, ſhe had a great ſenſe of God's love, and a glorious ſight, as if ſhe had ſeen the very heavens open, and the angels come to receive her, by which her heart was filled with joy, and her tongue with praiſe.

17. Being deſired by the ſtanders-by to give them a particular account of what ſhe ſaw, ſhe anſwered, "you ſhall know hereafter" and ſo in an extaſy of joy and holy triumph ſhe went to God, when ſhe was about twelve years old.

EXAMPLE

EXAMPLE IV.

1. CHARLES BRIDGEMAN had no fooner learned to fpeak, but he betook himfelf to prayer.

2. He was prone to learn the things of God.

3. He would be often teaching them their duty that waited upon him.

4. He learned by heart many good things before he was fit to go to fchool. and when he was at fchool: fo religious were his words, his actions fo upright, his devotions fo hearty, his fear of God fo great, that many were ready to fay, as they did of John, *What manner of child fhall this be?*

5. He would be much in reading the holy fcriptures.

6. He was defirous of more fpiritual knowledge, and would be often afking very ferious queftions.

7. He

7 He would not ſtir out of doors before he had poured out his ſoul to the Lord.

8 When he ate any thing, he would be ſure to lift up his heart unto the Lord for a bleſſing upon it, and when he had moderately refreſhed himſelf by eating, he would not forget to acknowledge God's goodneſs in feeding him.

9. He would not lie down in his bed till he had been upon his knees; and when ſometimes he had forgotten his duty, he would quickly get out of his bed, and kneeling down upon his bare knees, aſk God forgiveneſs for that ſin.

10 He would rebuke his brethren, if at any time they were haſty at their meals, or eat without aſking a bleſſing. His check was uſually this, *Dare you do this? God be merciful to us; this bit of bread might choak us.*

11. His ſentences were wiſe and weighty, and might well become an ancient Chriſtian.

12. His ſickneſs was lingering; in which one told him of poſſeſſions that muſt fall to his portion, and what are they? ſaid he *I had rather have the kingdom of heaven than a thouſand ſuch inheritances*

13. When he was ſick, he ſeemed much taken up with heaven, aſking very ſerious queſtions about the nature of his ſoul.

14. After he was pretty well ſatisfied about that, he enquired how his ſoul might be ſaved? The anſwer being made "by the applying of Chriſt's merits by faith," he was pleaſed with the anſwer, and was ready to give any one that ſhould deſire it, an account of his hope

15. Being aſked whether he had rather live or die? He anſwered, *I deſire to die, that I may go to my Saviour.*

16. His

16 His pains increaſing, one aſked him, Whether he would rather ſtill endure thoſe pains or forſake Chriſt? "Alas, ſaid he, I know not what to ſay, being but a child: theſe pains may ſtagger a ſtrong man, but I will endure them the beſt that I can." Upon this he called to mind that martyr, Thomas Bilney; who being in priſon the night before his burning put his finger into the candle, to know how he could endure the fire, 'O! ſaid the child, had I lived then, I would have run through the fire to have gone to Chriſt.'"

17 Three days before his death he told them not only that he muſt die, but the day no ſooner was that day come, but he fell into a trance, his eyes were fixed, his face cheerful, his hands and arms claſped in a bow, as if he would have received ſome bleſſed angels that were at hand to receive his ſoul. When he

he came to himſelf, he told them how he ſaw the ſweeteſt body that ever eyes beheld, who bid him be of good cheer, for he muſt preſently go with him.

18 The laſt words he ſpake, were theſe: "Pray, pray, pray, nay, yet pray, and the more prayers the better all proſpers God is the beſt phyſician; into thy hands I commend my ſpirit. O Lord Jeſus, receive my ſoul. Now cloſe mine eyes. Forgive me father, mother, brothers, ſiſters, all the world. Now I am well, my pain is almoſt gone, my joy is at hand. Lord have mercy on me. O Lord receive my ſoul unto thee" And thus he yielded up his ſpirit unto the Lord, when he was about twelve years old.

EXAMPLE V.

1. A Very poor child of the pariſh of Newington-Butts, came to the door of a friend of mine, in a very lamentable caſe it pleaſed God to raiſe in the heart of my friend, a great pity and tenderneſs toward him; ſo that he took him out of the ſtreets who had nothing at all to commend him to any one's charity but his miſery,. My friend eyeing the glory of God, diſcharged the pariſh of the child, and took him as his own, yet there ſeemed to be little hopes of doing good upon him, for he was a very monſter of wickedneſs, and a thouſand times more miſerable and vile by his ſin, than by his poverty. He was running to hell as ſoon as he could go, and was old in vice when he was young in years, one ſhall ſcarce hear of one

one ſo like the devil in his infancy, as this poor child was What ſin was there (that his age was capable of) that he did not commit? What by the corruption of his nature, and the abominable example of little beggar-boys, he was arrived to a ſtrong pitch of impiety. He would call names, take God's name in vain, curſe and ſwear, and do almoſt all kinds of miſchief; and as to any thing of God, was worſe than a heathen.

2. No ſooner had this good man taken this creature into his houſe, but he prayed for him, and laboured with all his might to convince him of his miſerable condition by nature, and to teach him ſome thing of God, the worth of his own ſoul, and that eternity of glory or miſery that he was born to. And bleſſed be God, it was not long before the Lord was pleaſed to let him underſtand, that it was himſelf which put

put it into his heart to take in this child. The Lord soon struck in with his instructions, so that an amazing change was seen. In a few weeks space he was convinced of the evil of his ways, no more calling of names, swearing or cursing; no more taking of the Lord's name in vain. His company, his talk, his employment were changed, and he was like another creature.

3. And this change was not only an external one, but he would get by himself, and weep and mourn bitterly for his wicked life.

4. He was still more and more broken under a sense of his undone state by nature: oft in tears, and bemoaning his lost and miserable condition. When his master spoke of the things of God, he listened earnestly, and took in, with much greediness and affection, what he was taught. Seldom was there any discourse about religion in his hearing,

 but

but he heard as if it were for his life.

5. Thus he continued feeking after the knowledge of God, till the ficknefs came into the houfe, with which he was fmitten. At his firft fickening, the poor child was greatly amazed and afraid, and thought his pains were great and the diftemper very tedious, yet the fenfe of his fin, and the thought of the condition his foul was ftill in, made his trouble ten times greater. He was in grievous agonies of fpirit, and his former fins ftared him in his face and made him tremble. The poifon of God's arrows did even drink up his fpirits, the fenfe of fin and wrath was fo great, that he could not tell what to do. The weight of God's difpleafure, and the thoughts of lying under it to all eternity, did even break him to pieces, and he cried out bitterly, What fhould he do? He was a miferable finner, and he feared that he fhould go to hell!

His

His ſins had been ſo great and ſo many, that there was no hope for him. He was not by far ſo much concerned for his life as for his ſoul, what would become of that for ever Now the plague upon his body ſeemed nothing to that which was in his ſoul.

6 He not only cried out of himſelf, for his ſwearing and lying, and other outwardly notorious ſins, but was in great horror for the ſin of his nature, for the vileneſs of his heart, and original corruption For this he was in ſo great anguiſh that the trouble of his ſpirit made him forget the pains of his body.

7. He did very particularly confeſs and bewail his ſins, and ſome ſins ſo ſecret, that none in the world could charge him with.

8. He would aſk others whether they thought there were any hopes for him, and would beg of them to deal plainly with him, for he was greatly afraid of being deceived.*

C H A P.

9. Being informed how willing and ready the Lord Christ was to accept of poor sinners, and being counselled to venture himself upon Christ for mercy and salvation, he said, he would fain cast himself upon Christ, but he could not but wonder how Christ should die for such a vile wretch as he was and he found it one of the hardest things in the world to believe.

10. But at last it pleased the Lord to give him some hope that their might be mercy for him, the chief of sinners, and he was enabled to lay hold upon that, *Come unto me all ye that are weary and heavy laden, and I will give you rest* Nor was it long before he was full of praise, and admiration of God, so that (to speak in the words of one that was an eye and ear-witness) the house at that day, for all the sickness in it, was like a little, lower heaven, so full of joy and praise.

11. He

11. He now grew exceedingly in knowledge, experience, patience, humility, and felf abhorrency He prayed before but now the Lord poured out upon him the fpirit of prayer in an extraordinary manner: fo that now he prayed more frequently, more earneftly, more fpiritually than ever O how eagerly would he beg to be wafhed in the blood of Jefus! And that the King of kings, and Lord of lords, who was over heaven and earth, would pardon and forgive him all his fins, and receive his foul into his kingdom And what he fpoke, was with fo much life and fervor of fpirit, that it filled the hearers with aftonifhment and joy.

12 He had no fmall fenfe of the ufe and excellency of Chrift, and fuch longing and breathings of his foul after him, that when mention had been made of Chrift, he hath been

been ready to leap out of his bed for joy.

13. The Wednesday before he died, he lay as it were in a trance for about half an hour, in which time he thought he saw a vision of angels: when he was out of his trance, he asked his nurse why she did not let him go? Go whither child! said she. Why along with those brave gentlemen, said he; but they told me they would come and fetch me away upon Friday. And he doubled his words many times, upon Friday next, those brave gentlemen will come for me.

14. He was very thankful to his master, and very sensible of his great kindness, in taking him out of the streets, when he was begging; and he admired the goodness of God, which put it into the mind of a stranger, to look upon such a pitiful creature as he was. "O my dear master (said he) I hope to see

you

you in heaven, for I am ſure you will go thither. O bleſſed, bleſſed be God, that made you to take pity upon me for I might have died, and have gone to the devil, and been damned for ever, if it had not been for you"

15 The Thurſday before he died, he aſked a friend of mine, what he thought of his condition, and whither his ſoul was going? For he ſaid he could not ſtill but fear, leſt he ſhould deceive himſelf with falſe hopes. At which my friend ſpoke to him thus, If thou art but willing to accept of him, thou mayeſt have Chriſt and all that thou doſt want with him. Thou ſayeſt, thou feareſt that Chriſt will not accept of thee: I fear thou art not heartily willing to accept of him. The child anſwered, Indeed I am 'Why then, if thou art unfeignedly willing to have Chriſt, I tell thee, he is a thouſand times more willing to

have thee, and wash thee, and save thee. And now at this time Christ offers himself freely to thee again; therefore receive him humbly by faith into thy heart, and bid him welcome, for he deserveth it." Upon which words, the Lord discovered his love to the child, and he gave a kind of a leap in his bed, and snapt his fingers and thumb together with abundance of joy. And from that time forward, in full joy, and assurance of God's love, he continued earnestly praising God, desiring to die and be with Christ. And on Friday morning he sweetly went to rest, using that expression, *Into thy hands, Lord, I commit my spirit*, being not much above nine years old.

EXAMPLE VI.

JOHN SUDLOW was born of religious parents, in the county of

of Middlesex, whose great care was to instil spiritual principles into him as soon as he was capable of understanding them whose endeavours the Lord was pleased to crown with the desired success

2. When he was scarce able to speak plain, he seemed to have a very great awe and reverence of God upon his spirit, and a strange sense of the things of another world.

3 The first thing that much affected him and made him endeavour to escape from the wrath to come, and to enquire what he should do to be saved, was the death of a little brother. When he saw him without breath, and not able to speak or stir, and when carried out of doors, and put into the ground, he was greatly concerned, and asked, "Whether he should die too?" Being answered, Yes, it made such a deep impression upon him, that from that time forward, he was exceeding

ceeding ſerious, and this was when he was about four years old.

4. He was now deſirous to know what he might do that he might live in another world, and what avoid, that he might not die for ever. And being inſtructed by his parents, he ſoon laboured to avoid whatſoever might diſpleaſe God. Now the apprehenſions of God, and death, and eternity, laid ſuch a reſtraint upon him, that he would not for a world have told a lie.

5. He was much taken with the reading of the book of Martyrs, and would willingly leave his dinner to go to his book.

6. He went to his father and mother with great tenderneſs and compaſſion, and begged of them to take more care of the ſouls of his brethren and ſiſters, and to take heed leſt they ſhould go to hell and be ruined for ever.

7. The providences of God were not passed by without considerable observations by him.

8. In the time of the plague he was exceedingly concerned about his everlasting state, and was very much by himself upon his knees. This prayer was found written in short-hand after his death.

O LORD GOD *and merciful Father, take pity upon me, a miserable sinner and strengthen me O Lord in thy faith, and make me one of thy glorious saints in heaven O Lord, keep me from this poisonous infection, however, not my will, but thy will be done O Lord if thou hast appointed me to die by it, fit me for death, and give me a good heart to bear up under my afflictions. O Lord God, and merciful Father, take pity on me, thy child, teach me, O Lord, thy word, make me strong in faith. O Lord, I have sinned against thee: Lord, pardon my sins. I had been in*

hell

hell long ago if it had not been for thy mercy. But O Lord, if thou hast appointed me to die, fit me for death, that I may die with comfort. And O Lord, I pray thee to help me bear up under all my afflictions, for Christ his sake. Amen.

9. He was not a little concerned for the whole nation, and begged that God would pardon the sins of this land, and bring it nearer to himself.

10. About the beginning of November, 1695, this child was smote with the distemper, but he behaved with admirable patience under the hand of God.

18 These were some of his last expressions —The Lord shall be my physician, for he will cure both soul and body—Heaven is the best hospital—*It is the Lord, let him do what seemeth good in his eyes* Again, It is the Lord that taketh away my health;

health; but I will ſay as Job did, *Bleſſed be the name of the Lord* If I ſhould live longer I ſhould but ſin againſt God Looking upon his father he ſaid, if the Lord will but lend me the leaſt finger of his hand, to lead me through the dark entry of death, I will rejoice in him

12. When a miniſter came to him, among other things, he ſpake ſomewhat of life. He ſaid, this is a wicked world, it is better to live in heaven

13 An hour and a half before his death, the ſame miniſter came again to viſit him, and aſked him, John art thou not afraid to die? He anſwered No, if the Lord will but comfort me in that hour. But, ſaid the miniſter, how canſt thou expect comfort, ſeeing we deſerve none? He anſwered, No, if I had my deſerts, I had been in hell long ago. But, replied the miniſter,

which way doſt thou expect comfort and ſalvation, ſeeing thou art a ſinner? He anſwered, in Chriſt alone ——In whom, about an hour and a half after, he fell aſleep.

EXAMPLE VII.

1. TABITHA ALDER was the daughter of a Miniſter in Kent, who lived near Graveſend. She was inſtructed in the holy ſcriptures, by her father and mother but there appeared nothing extraordinary in her, till ſhe was between ſeven and eight years old.

2. About which time when ſhe was ſick, one aſked her, what ſhe thought would become of her, if ſhe ſhould die? She anſwered, That ſhe was greatly afraid ſhe ſhould go to hell.

3 Being aſked, Why ſhe was afraid ſhe ſhould go to hell? She anſwered,

anſwered, becauſe ſhe did not love God

4 Again, being aſked how ſhe knew that ſhe did not love God? She replied, "What have I done for God ever ſince I was born? And beſide this, I have been taught, that he that loves God, keeps his commandments, but I have kept none of them at all."

5 Being further demanded, if ſhe would not fain love God? She anſwered, Yes, with all her heart if ſhe could, but ſhe found it a hard thing to love one ſhe did not ſee.

6 She was adviſed to beg of God a heart to love him ſhe anſwered ſhe was afraid it was too late

7 Upon this, ſeeing her in ſuch a deſponding condition, a friend of her's ſpent the next day in faſting and prayer for her.

8. After this, that friend aſked her, how ſhe did now? She anſwered,

ſwered, with a great deal of joy, That now ſhe bleſſed the Lord ſhe loved the Lord Jeſus dearly, ſhe felt ſhe did love him, O, ſaid ſhe I love him dearly.

9. Why, ſaid her friend, did you not ſay yeſterday, you did not love the Lord, and that you could not? "Sure (ſaid ſhe) it was Satan hindered. But now I love him O bleſſed be God for the Lord Jeſus Chriſt."

10. After this ſhe had a diſcovery of her approaching diſſolution, which was no ſmall comfort to her "Anon (ſaid ſhe with a holy triumph) I ſhall be with Jeſu. I am married to him, he is my huſband I am his bride, I have given myſelf to him, and he hath given himſelf to me, and I ſhall live with him for ever."

11. This language made the hearers ſtand aſtoniſhed. ſhe continued in a kind of extaſy of joy, admiring

ing the excellency of Chrift, rejoicing in her intereft in him, and longing to be with him.

12 After awhile fome of her friends ftanding by her, obferved a more than ordinary earneftnefs and fixednefs in her countenance; they faid one to another, Look how earneftly fhe looks, fure fhe feeth fomething.

13 One afked what it was fhe fixed her eyes upon fo eagerly? I warrant, faith one, fhe feeth death a coming.

14 No, faid fhe, it is the glory that I fee, it is that I fix my eye upon

15. One afked her, What was the glory like? She anfwered, "I cannot fpeak what, but I am going to it, will you go with me? I am going to glory O that all you were to go with me to that glory," With which words her

ſoul took wing, and went to the poſſeſſion of that glory. She died when ſhe was between eight and nine years old.

EXAMPLE VIII.

1. SUSAN [illegible] BICKS was born at Leyden in Holland, Jan 24, 1650, of religious parents, whoſe great care was to inſtruct their child, and to preſent her to the miniſters of the place to be publicly inſtructed.

2. It pleaſed God to bleſs th[illegible] to her ſoul, ſo that ſhe had ſoon a true reliſh of what ſhe was taught, and made an admirable uſe of it in time of need.

3. She was a child of great dutifulneſs to her parents, and of a very ſweet, humble nature, and not only the truth, but the power and eminency of religion did ſhine in her.

4. In

4 In the month of Auguſt, 1664, when the peſtilence raged in Holland, as ſhe felt herſelf very ill, ſhe broke forth into theſe words; *If thy law were not my delight, I ſhould periſh in my affliction.*

5 Her father coming to her, ſaid, "Be of good comfort, my child, for the Lord will be near to thee and us; he will not forſake us, though he chaſten us." 'Yea, father, ſaid ſhe, our heavenly Father doth chaſten us for our profit, that we may be partakers of his holineſs; no chaſtiſement ſeemeth for the preſent to be joyous, but grievous, but afterwards it yieldeth the peaceable fruits of righteouſneſs to them which are exerciſed thereby.'

6 After this, with her eyes lift up to heaven, ſhe ſaid, *Be merciful to me O Father, be merciful to me a ſinner, according to thy word.*

7. She

7 She was a great hater of sin, and did with much grief and self-abhorrence reflect upon it, but that which lay most upon her heart, was the corruption of her nature. Oft would she cry out in the words of the Psalmist, *Behold I was shapen in iniquity, and in sin did my mother conceive me.* She could never lay herself low enough under a sense of that sin which she brought with her into the world.

8 That scripture was much in her mouth, *The sacrifices of God are a contrite heart, a broken and contrite spirit, O God thou wilt not despise.* "O for that brokenness of heart, said she, which flows from faith, and for that faith which is built upon Christ, who is the proper and alone sacrifice for sin."

9. Then she discoursed of the nature of faith, and desired that the eleventh of the Hebrews should be

be read unto her: at the reading of which ſhe cried out, "O what a ſtedfaſt faith was Abraham's, which made him willing to offer up his own and only ſon! *Faith is indeed the ſubſtance of things hoped for, the evidence of things not ſeen.*"

10. Her father and mother hearing her, burſt out into tears; upon which ſhe pleadeth with them to be patient under the hand of God. "O, ſaid ſhe, why do you weep over me, ſeeing you have no reaſon to queſtion, but if the Lord take me, it ſhall be well with me to all eternity? You ought to be well ſatisfied, ſeeing it is ſaid, *God is in heaven, and doth whatſoever pleaſeth him.* And do you not pray every day, that the will of God may be done upon earth as it is done in heaven? Now, father, this is God's will, that I ſhould lie upon this ſick bed, and of this diſeaſe, ſhall

we not be content when our prayers are answered? I will, as long as I live, pray that God's will be done not mine."

11 "Doth not, said she, the pestilence come from God? Why else doth the scripture say, *Shall they be evil in the city which I have not sent?* Does it come from the air? And is not the Lord the creator and ruler of the air? Or if they say, it comes from the earth, hath not he the same power and influence upon that too? What talk they of a ship that came from Africa? Have ye not heard long ago, *I will bring a sword upon you, and avenge the quarrel of my covenant, and when you are assembled in the cities then I will bring the pestilence in the midst of you?*"

12 After this, having taken a little rest, she said, "Whether in death or life a believer is Christ's, who

who hath redeemed us by his own precious blood from the power of the devil then whether I live or die, I am the Lord's. O why do you afflict yourselves thus! But what shall I say? With weeping I came into the world, and with weeping I must go out again, O my dear parents, better is the day of my death than the day of my birth."

13 She then desired her father to pray with her, and to request of the Lord, that she might have a quiet passage into another world.

14. Her father perceiving her to grow very weak, said, "I perceive, child, thou art very weak." "It is true, Sir said she, I feel my weakness increased, and I see your sorrow increasing too, which is a piece of my affliction. Be content, I pray you, it is the Lord which doth it, and let you and I say with

David, *Let us fall into the Lord's hands, for his mercies are great.*

15. She had a great check upon her passions now, [illegible] after her death, urging that of David, while the child was sick, he fasted and wept but when he died, he washed his face and sat up and eat and said, *Can I bring him back from death? I shall go to him, but he shall not return to me.*

16. Being very feeble, she said, "O that I might quietly sleep in the bosom of Jesus! and that till then he would strengthen me! O that he would take me in his arms, as he did those little ones where he said *Suffer little children to come unto me, for of such is the kingdom of heaven, and he took them in his arms, and laid his hands on them, and blessed them.* I lie here as a child, O Lord, I am thy child receive me into thy gracious arms.

O Lord,

O Lord, grace! grace! and not justice! For if thou shouldest enter into judgment with me, I cannot [illegible] none living should be [illegible]

[illegible] she said, "O what is the [illegible]! *The days of man upon the [illegible] and as the flower of the [illegible] he flourisheth, the wind [illegible] over it, and it is gone, and its place knows her no more.*

18 She added, my life [illegible] not continue [illegible] I feel much weakness. O Lord, look upon me graciously, [illegible] pity upon my weak, [illegible] I am oppressed [illegible] for me, that I may [illegible] overcome.

19 She was very frequent in spiritual [illegible], and it was no small comfort to her that the Lord Christ did pray for her, and promise to send his Spirit to comfort

fort her. "It is said, said she, *I will pray the Father, and he shall give you another Comforter.* O let him not leave me! O Lord, continue with me till my battle and work is finished!"

20. Soon after, she said, "None but Christ! Without thee I can do nothing! Christ is the true vine: O let me be a branch of that vine! What poor worms are we! O dear father, how lame and halting do we go on in the ways of God and salvation? We know but in part, but when that which is perfect is come, then that which is imperfect shall be done away. O that I had attained to that now! But what are we ourselves? Not only weakness and nothingness, but wickedness: for all the thoughts and imaginations of man's heart are only evil, and that continually; we are by nature children of wrath,

and

and are conceived in sin and born in unrighteousness. O! this wretched and vile thing sin! But thanks be to God who hath redeemed me from it. O Lord, take me to thyself. Behold, dear mother, he hath prepared a place for me."

21. "Yea, my dear child, said her mother, he shall strengthen you with his Holy Spirit, until he hath fitted and prepared you fully for that place which he hath prepared for you."

22. "Yea, mother, replied she, it is said in the 84th Psalm, *How lovely are thy Tabernacles, O Lord of hosts, my soul doth thirst, and long for the courts of the Lord: one day in thy courts is better than a thousand; yea, I had rather be a door-keeper in the house of my God, than dwell in the tents of the wicked.* Read that Psalm dear mother, wherewith we may comfort one another.

another. As for me, I am more and more spent, and draw near my last hour.'

Then she quoted Job's words: *I know that my Re[illegible]er liveth, and that he shall stand at the latter day upon the earth; and though [illegible] destroy this body, yet in my flesh shall I see God.*

Then she said, "*Marvel not at this, for the hour is coming, in which all that are in the graves shall hear his voice, and come forth; they that have done good, unto the resurrection of life.* See, father, I shall rise in that day, and then I shall behold my Redeemer; then shall he say, *Come ye blessed of my Father, inherit the kingdom prepared for you from the beginning of the world. Behold now I live, yet not I, but Christ liveth in me, and the life that I now live in the flesh, is by the* [illegible] *faith of the Son of God, who loved me and gave himself for me. I am saved and that not of myself, it is the gift of God, not of works, lest any man should boast.*

My dear parents, now we must part my speech faileth me: pray to the Lord for a quiet close to my combat Her parents replied, "My dear child! how sad is that to us, that we must part?" She answered "I go to heaven and there we shall find one another again. I go to Jesus Christ"

26. Then she comforted herself to think of her precious brother and sister. "I go to my brother Jacob, who did so much cry and call upon God to the last moment of his breath and to my little sister who was but three years old, when she died who when we asked her, whether she would die? a [illegible] if it be the Lord's will.

will. I will go to my little brother, if it be the Lord's will, or I will ſtay with my mother, if it be the Lord's will. But I know that I ſhall die and go to heaven."

27. After this, her ſpirit was refreſhed with the ſenſe of the pardon of her ſins, which made her to cry out, "Behold, God hath waſhed away my ſins. O now do I long to die The Lord is my ſhepherd although I paſs through the valley of the ſhadow of death I will not fear, for thou art with me ſhall I not ſuffer, ſeeing my glorious Redeemer was pleaſed to ſuffer ſo much for me? O now was he mocked and crowned with thorns, that he might purchaſe a crown of righteouſneſs for us! Muſt I not exalt and bleſs him while I have a being, who hath bought me, even with his blood? Behold the Lamb of God, that

taketh

taketh away the ſins of the world! That Lamb is Jeſus Chriſt, who hath ſatisfied for my ſins."

28 My end is now very near, now I ſhall put on the white raiment, and be clothed before the Lamb, that ſpotleſs Lamb, and with his ſpotleſs righteouſneſs Now are the angels making ready to carry my ſoul before the throne of God. "Theſe are they who are come out of great tribulation, who have waſhed their robes, and made them white in the blood of the Lamb." She ſpoke this with a dying voice but full of ſpirit and of the power of faith

29. Her lively aſſurance ſhe further uttered in the words of the apoſtle. *We know that if this earthly houſe of our tabernacle be diſſolved, we have a building of God, which is eternal in the heavens for in this we*

ſigh

ſigh for our houſe, which is in heaven, that we may be clothed therewith

30. There, father, you ſee that my body is this tabernacle, which now ſhall be broken down, my ſoul ſhall now part from it, and ſhall be taken up in paradiſe, into that heavenly Jeruſalem There ſhall I dwell and go no more out, but ſit and ſing, holy, holy, is the Lord God of hoſts, the Lord of Sabbaoth! Her laſt words were theſe, "O Lord God, into thy hands I commit my ſpirit O Lord be gracious, be merciful to me a poor ſinner."

31 She died the firſt of September, 1664, betwixt ſeven and eight in the evening, in the fourteenth year of her age.

EXAMPLE IX.

1. JACOB BICKS the brother of Susannah Bicks, was born in Leyden, in the year 1657 He was visited with sickness, upon the sixth of August, 1664, three or four weeks before his sister In his distemper he was very sleepy, till near his death but when he did awake he was wont still to fall a pray r

2. Once when his parents had prayed with him, they asked him, if they should once more send for the physician? No said he, I will have the doctor no more, the Lord will help me I know he will take me to himself.

3 When his parents had prayed with him, he said. "Come now,

dear

dear father and mother, and kiſs me, I know that I ſhall die. Farewel, dear father and mother; farewel, dear ſiſter, farewel all. Now ſhall I go unto God and Jeſus Chriſt, and the holy angels. Father, know you not what is ſaid by Jeremiah? *Bleſſed is he who truſteth in the Lord* Now I truſt in him, and he will bleſs me. And in 1 John ii. it is ſaid *Little children, love not the world for the world paſſeth away.*"

4 "Away then all that is in the world away with all my pleaſant things in the world, away with my digger, for where I go there is nothing to do with daggers and ſwords. Men ſhall not fight there, but praiſe God Away with all my books, there ſhall I learn true wiſdom without books."

5. His

5. His father faid, "My dear child, the Lord will be near thee, and uphold thee."

6 'Yea, father (faid he) the apoftle Peter faith *God refifteth the proud, but he giveth grace to the humble* I humble myfelf under the mighty hand of God, and he fhall help me, and lift me up"

7. "O, my dear child, (faid his father) haft thou fo ftrong faith?"

8 'Yes faid he, God hath given me fo ftrong a faith in himfelf through Jefus Chrift, that the devil fhall flee from me. for it is faid *He who believeth in the Son hath everlafting life and he hath overcome the wicked one.* Now I believe in Jefus Chrift, my Redeemer, and he will not leave nor forfake me, but fhall give unto me eternal life, and then I fhall fing, *Holy, holy, holy is the Lord of Sabbaoth.*"

9. Then

9 Then with that word, "Lord, be merciful unto me a poor ſinner," he quietly breathed out his ſoul, being about ſeven years old.

EXAMPLE X.

1. JOHN HARVEY was born in London, in the year 1655, his father was a Dutch merchant: he was piouſly educated under his mother, and ſoon began to hear divine things with delight.

2. The firſt thing obſervable in him, was, that when he was two years and eight months old he could ſpeak as well as other children do uſually at five years old.

3. His parents judging, that he was then too young to ſend to ſchool, let him have his liberty to play about their yard, but inſtead of

of playing, he found out a ſchool of his own accord near home, and went to the ſchool-miſtreſs, and intreated her to teach him to read, and ſo he went for ſome time to ſchool without the knowledge of his parents, and made a very ſtrange progreſs in his learning and was able to read diſtinctly, before moſt children know their letters

4. He was wont to aſk many ſerious and weighty queſtions about matters which concerned his ſoul and eternity

5 His mother being greatly troubled upon the death of one of his uncles, this child came to his mother, and ſaid, "Mother, though my uncle be dead, doth not the ſcripture ſay he muſt riſe again? Yes and I muſt die, and ſo muſt every body, and it will not be long before Chriſt will come

to judge the world, and then we ſhall ſee one another again, I pray mother, do not weep ſo much" He was not then quiet five years old: by which her ſorrow for her brother was turned into admiration, and ſhe was made to ſi ſilent and quiet under that trying providence.

6. After this his parents removed to Aberdeen and ſettled their child under a ſchool maſt r there, whoſe cuſtom was upon the Lord's-day in the morning to examine his ſcholars, concerning the ſermons they had heard the former Lord's-day, and to add ſome other queſtions which might try the underſtanding and knowledge of his ſcholars The queſtion that was once propoſed to his form was, Whether God had a mother? None of the ſcholars could anſwer it, till it came to John Harvey, who being

aſked,

asked, Whether God had a mother? Answered, No; as he was God, he could not have a mother; but as he was man he had. This was before he was six years old.

7 One day, seeing one of his near relations come into his father's house distempered with drink, he went to him, and wept over him, and besought him that he would not so offend God, and hazard his soul.

8 He was a conscientious observer of the Lord's-day, spending all the time either in secret prayer, reading the scriptures and good books, learning his catechism, or hearing the word of God. And he was not only careful in the performance of these duties himself, but was ready to put all that he knew upon a strict observation of the Lord's day.

9. He

9. He was very humble and modeſt, and hated any thing more than neceſſaries either in clothes or diet.

10. When he perceived either his brother or ſiſter pleaſed with their new clothes, he would reprove their folly, and when his reproof ſignified little, he would bewail their vanity.

11. Once he had a new ſuit brought from the taylor's, which, when he looked on, he found ſome ribbons at the knees, at which he was grieved, aſking his mother, "Whether thoſe things would keep him warm?" No, child, ſaid his mother. "Why then ſaid he, do you ſuffer them to be put here? You are miſtaken if you think ſuch things pleaſe me; and, I doubt, ſome that are better than us may

want

want the mony, that this coſt you; to buy them bread.

12 At leiſure times he was talking to his ſchool-fellows about the things of God, and the neceſſity of a holy life. That text he much ſpoke on to them, *The axe is laid to the root of the tree, and every tree that bringeth not forth good fruit, is hewn down and caſt into the fire.*

13. After this his parents removed not far from London, where he continued till the year ſixty-five. He was then ſent to the Latin ſchool, where he ſoon made a very conſiderable progreſs, and was greatly beloved of his maſter. The ſchool was his beloved place, and learning his recreation.

14 He had a word to ſay to every one that he converſed with, to put them in mind of the worth of Chriſt and their ſouls and their

nearneſs

nearneſs to eternity, inſomuch that good people took no ſmall pleaſure in his company.

15. He bewailed the miſerable condition of the generality of mankind, (when he was about ten years old) that they were utterly eſtranged from God. "Though they called him father, he ſaid, yet they were his children by creation, and not by any likeneſs they had to God, or any intereſt in him."

16. Thus he continued walking in the ways of God, in reading, praying, hearing the word of God, and ſpiritual diſcourſe, diſcovering thereby his ſerious thoughts of eternity; which ſeemed to ſwallow up all other thoughts, and he lived in a conſtant preparation for it, and looked more like one that was ripe for glory than an inhabitant of the lower world.

17. When he was about eleven years and three quarters old, his mother's houſe was viſited with a plague, his eldeſt ſiſter was the firſt that was viſited with this diſtemper, and when they were praying for her, he would ſob and weep bitterly.

18. As ſoon as he perceived his ſiſter was dead, he ſaid, "*The will of the Lord be done: bleſſed be the Lord!* Dear Mother, you muſt do as David did, after the child was dead he went and refreſhed himſelf, and quietly ſubmitted to the will of God."

19. The reſt of the family held well for ſome days which time he ſpent in preparing for death. Mean time he wrote ſeveral meditations, upon ſeveral ſubjects, particularly upon the excellency of Chriſt. He was never well, but when he was

more

more immediately engaged in the ſervice of God.

20. At fourteen days end, he was taken ſick, at which he ſeemed very cheerful though his pains were great.

21 His mother looking upon his brother, ſhaked her head. at which he aſked if his brother were marked? She anſwered "Yea child." He aſked again, Whether he were marked? She anſwered nothing. "Well, ſays he, I know I ſhall be marked I pray let me have Mr Baxter's book, that I may read a little more of eternity before I go into it" His mother told him, he was not able to read. He ſaid, "then pray by me and for me"

22 His mother aſked him, whether he was willing to die and leave her? He anſwered, "Yes, I am

am willing to leave you, and go to my heavenly Father." She anſwered, "Child, if thou hadſt but an aſſurance of God's love, I ſhould not be ſo much troubled." He anſwered, "I am aſſured that my ſins are forgiven, and that I ſhall go to heaven for, ſaid he, here ſtood an angel by me, that told me I ſhould quickly be in glory."

23. At this his mother burſt forth into tears. "O mother, ſaid he, did you but know what joy I feel, you would not weep but rejoice. I tell you I am ſo full of comfort, that I cannot tell you how I am: O mother, I ſhall preſently have my head in my Father's boſom, and ſhall be there where the *four and twenty elders caſt down their crowns, and ſing Hallelujah, glory, and praiſe, to him that ſits upon the throne, and to the Lamb for ever!*"

24. Upon

24. Upon this his speech began to fail him, but his soul was still taken up with glory, and nothing now grieved him, but the sorrow that he saw his mother to be in for his death a little to divert her, he asked, "What she had for supper?" But presently in a kind of rapture, he cried out, "O what a sweet supper have I making ready for me in glory"

25 But seeing all this did but increase his mother's grief he asked her, "What she meant thus to offend God? Know you not that it is the hand of the Almighty? *Humble yourself under the mighty hand of God*, lay yourself in the dust, and kiss the rod in token of your submission to the will of God" Upon which, raising himself a little, he gave a lowly bow and spoke no more but went to rest in the bosom of Jesus.

FINIS.